MW01600503

WORKBOOK FOR PRACTICING THE WAY BY JOHN MARK COMER

Be with Jesus. Become Like Him.
Do as He Did.

(A Complementary Guide to Truly Follow Jesus)

Full Moon Press

BONUS: FREE AUDIOBOOK

Get Your Bonus Today!

As a thank you for your purchase, we would like to offer you the following gift completely free.

Scan the QR code or use the link below it to get your free audiobook now.

https://fullmoon.press/bonus-practicing-the-way/

DISCLAIMER

This book, "Workbook for Practicing the Way by John Mark Comer: Be with Jesus. Become Like Him. Do as He Did. (A Complementary Guide to Truly Follow Jesus)", is an independent creation and is not linked with the original publication, *Practicing the Way: Be with Jesus. Become Like Him. Do as He Did.*, by John Mark Comer. Even though this workbook acts as a complementary tool, it is not approved or authorized by the writer or publisher of the original book. Its purpose is to offer additional perspectives and activities to live life as Christ would.

This Workbook Belongs To:

Name:

Address:

Contact:

TABLE OF CONTENTS

HOW TO USE THIS WORKBOOK

Note: Before you start working on this workbook, it's highly suggested to read *Practicing the Way* by John Mark Comer. This book lays the foundation for insights, teachings, and exercises meant to assist you in truly following Jesus Christ. By diving into Comer's wisdom and guidance, you'll grasp the key concepts and principles behind the lessons in this workbook profoundly.

1. Read the introduction to get a better grasp of what this workbook is all about. Understand how it works alongside *Practicing the Way* by John Mark Comer and helps you on your journey to becoming formed by Jesus Christ.

2. Each chapter of this workbook corresponds to the chapters in *Practicing the Way*. Read through the Summaries and Key Takeaways to get a good grasp of the teachings in that chapter.

3. Apply the teachings by doing the exercises and answering the prompts in each chapter. Take your time, and go through these carefully and with intention. This is where your progress will be made!

4. Consider the additional exercises in the last chapter to really reinforce what you've learned.

5. Be consistent in using this workbook and embrace the journey. Engage with this workbook regularly and refer back to it after you have completed it to remind yourself of your objectives and to inspire you as you form your path to truly following Jesus.

INTRODUCTION

*"Because what you give your attention to is the person you become. Put another way: the mind is the portal to the soul, and what you fill your mind with will shape the trajectory of your character." - **John Mark Comer***

Welcome to a journey of transformation inspired by the profound teachings of John Mark Comer's *Practicing the Way: Be with Jesus. Become Like Him. Do as He Did.* This book has moved readers, opening their hearts and minds to the path of spiritual growth and deep connection with Jesus. However, reading powerful words and feeling inspired is only part of the equation; bringing those teachings into everyday life is where real change happens. That's where this workbook comes in.

Our purpose is clear: to be your practical companion in applying the rich insights from "Practicing the Way" into tangible actions that resonate in your daily existence. Think of this workbook as an extension of Comer's intentions, designed meticulously to help you integrate his teachings seamlessly. Here, you will find not just reflections but structured exercises that guide you in embodying the principles discussed in the book. The teachings of John Mark Comer are too impactful to be merely read and then shelved away. They urge us to transform, to become closer to Jesus, and to live out these truths in our mundane routines. This workbook serves as the bridge between inspiration and action, guiding you every step of the way towards creating a life deeply intertwined with Christ's presence.

As you delve into this workbook, you'll find it thoughtfully organized to lead you through various facets of spiritual growth imperative for building a Rule of Life—a concept central to Comer's approach. We start with the most foundational element: developing an intimate, personal relationship with Jesus. This isn't just about knowing of Jesus but experiencing Him, walking with Him in your everyday moments, and recognizing His presence in all aspects of your life. You'll encounter exercises designed to peel back the layers of superficial faith and dig deep into the roots of genuine, heartfelt connection.

Moving forward, we delve into character transformation. What does it truly mean to become like Jesus? It's more than adopting practices; it's about cultivating virtues akin to His. Patience, kindness, humility—these aren't traits we stumble upon but rather qualities we nurture through intentional practice. Here, you'll engage in reflective activities that challenge you to examine your character and align it more closely with Jesus' example. These chapters aren't just philosophical musings but pragmatic steps in shaping your inner life to mirror Christ's character.

The journey doesn't stop there. Living out your faith means engaging actively in Kingdom work. This involves understanding your unique role within God's grand narrative and acting on it. Whether it's through service, community involvement, or sharing the gospel, we guide you in identifying and stepping into this calling. The exercises provided here encourage not just contemplation but action—prompting you to move beyond your comfort zone and into meaningful participation in God's work.

Practicality is at the heart of this workbook. Each chapter is equipped with hands-on tools and exercises aimed at fostering real growth. Self-reflection exercises prompt you to look inward, honestly assessing your spiritual state. Goal-setting worksheets help you map out your aspirations in a concrete, achievable manner. Integration tasks ensure that you're not just thinking about spiritual disciplines but weaving them into your daily routine. Imagine the impact of consistently practicing gratitude, mindfulness, scripture meditation, and other disciplines Comer's teachings advocate. Through guided activities, these practices become less about tasks to complete and more about habits that naturally flow from a transformed heart.

This workbook is intentionally interactive, urging you to engage deeply and actively. Passive reading won't suffice here; real transformation requires effort and commitment. As you navigate through the sections, you'll be asked to jot down thoughts, reflect on experiences, set actionable goals, and track your progress. Such engagement ensures that the concepts don't remain abstract ideas but translate into lived realities. You will find blank spaces inviting you to pause and write, questions prompting you to think critically about your spiritual life, and checklists guiding you in implementing new habits.

The power of this workbook lies in its potential to transform. By systematically working through the exercises and integrating the lessons, you open yourself up to profound change. Imagine moving from a place of wanting to live like Jesus to actually doing so. Picture your day-to-day life infused with the peace, purpose, and joy that springs from a deeper connection with Christ. The aim is not perfection but progression—taking steady steps toward becoming who you are meant to be in God's eyes.

Your commitment to engaging with this workbook could mark a pivotal point in your spiritual journey. Every effort you make to apply these teachings adds a layer to your growth, making the abstract concrete and the theoretical practical. The transformation isn't instantaneous; it's gradual but significant. Each small step you take compounds over time, leading to substantial change.

In conclusion, this workbook invites you to an active, engaged process of spiritual growth. It complements John Mark Comer's "Practicing the Way" by offering you structured guidance in living out the principles he so eloquently presents. Your journey through these pages promises to be one of discovery, challenge, and ultimately, transformation. Engage deeply, act sincerely, and witness the profound changes that unfold as you move closer to living like Jesus in every aspect of your life. Welcome to a practical journey of faith, hope, and renewal.

CHAPTER 1
DUST

SUMMARY

In the chapter "Dust" from John Mark Comer's book "Practicing the Way," Comer delves into the concept of discipleship as it was understood in the context of first-century Jewish culture. The term "dust" refers to the idea of following a rabbi so closely that you would be covered in the dust kicked up by his feet. Comer emphasizes that modern Christians often miss this level of intimate, committed discipleship. He argues that being a disciple of Jesus means more than just intellectual assent or minimal religious participation; it involves a transformative process of becoming like Jesus in every aspect of life.

Comer illustrates this transformation through the concept of apprenticeship, where followers of Jesus are to be with Him, become like Him, and do the things He did. This involves integrating ancient Christian practices such as Sabbath, solitude, scripture reading, prayer, fasting, and community into daily life. Comer stresses that this journey requires intentionality, practical steps, and the support of a community, guiding readers to start small and gradually build up their spiritual disciplines. Ultimately, he highlights that true discipleship leads to a fuller, more purposeful life aligned with Jesus' teachings and examples.

KEY TAKEAWAYS

These takeaways underscore the profound commitment and intimacy required in discipleship, encouraging believers to closely follow and imitate Jesus in all aspects of life.

- Comer emphasizes the ancient Jewish context of discipleship, where being a disciple (talmid) meant following a rabbi so closely that one would be "covered in the dust" of the rabbi's feet. This metaphor illustrates the intimate and rigorous nature of true discipleship, highlighting the importance of closely observing and imitating Jesus in every aspect of life.

- The chapter underscores the transformative power of spending time with Jesus. By being in His presence and learning from His ways, disciples are gradually transformed to become more like Him. Comer encourages readers to prioritize being with Jesus through spiritual disciplines such as prayer, scripture reading, and worship.

- Comer portrays discipleship as a lifelong journey that requires dedication and perseverance. He encourages believers to commit to the continuous process of learning from Jesus, growing in character, and aligning their lives with His teachings. This commitment involves not only intellectual understanding but also practical application and heartfelt devotion.

EXERCISES/PROMPTS: REFLECTING ON DISCIPLESHIP AND FOLLOWING CLOSELY IN THE DUST OF JESUS

Use these prompts to deepen your understanding of what it means to follow Jesus closely and to reflect on how you can live out this commitment in practical ways.

Understanding Discipleship

Reflect on the metaphor of being "covered in the dust" of Jesus. What does this image evoke for you in terms of your relationship with Him?

_____

_____

_____

_____

_____

_____

_____

_____

_____

_____

_____

_____

How do you currently follow Jesus in your daily life? Are there specific areas where you feel you could draw closer to Him?

Transformative Proximity

Describe a time when being close to Jesus (through prayer, scripture, or worship) led to a significant change in your thoughts, behaviors, or attitudes. What was that experience like?

List some spiritual disciplines or practices that help you stay close to Jesus. How can you incorporate these more regularly into your routine?

Commitment to the Journey

Reflect on your personal journey of discipleship. In what ways have you grown to become more like Jesus so far? What areas still need growth?

Set a specific goal for your discipleship journey. What is one practical step you can take this week to follow Jesus more closely and to let His presence transform you?

CHAPTER 2
APPRENTICE TO JESUS

SUMMARY

In the chapter "Apprentice to Jesus" from "Practicing the Way" by John Mark Comer, the author explores the concept of discipleship through the lens of apprenticeship. Comer emphasizes that to truly follow Jesus means to be with him, become like him, and do as he did. He critiques the common view of Jesus as merely a historical figure or a symbol for moral inspiration, advocating instead for seeing Jesus as a highly intelligent and practical teacher whose insights into human flourishing are unparalleled. Comer insists that modern Christians often fail to respect Jesus as a guide for contemporary issues, preferring to follow cultural influencers instead.

Comer outlines the traditional Jewish system of education to illustrate the rigor and depth of discipleship in Jesus' time. He explains how Jewish children would memorize the Torah and, for the best students, continue to study the rest of the Hebrew Scriptures. This historical context sets the stage for understanding discipleship as a comprehensive and immersive practice. Jesus, as a rabbi, called his followers not just to learn from his teachings but to adopt his way of life entirely, much like apprentices learning a trade from a master craftsman.

The chapter further details how apprentices of Jesus should engage in nine key practices: Sabbath, solitude, scripture, generosity, prayer, community, fasting, witness, and service. These practices are intended to shape one's life around the principles and actions of Jesus. Comer stresses the importance of these practices being relational and habitual rather than perfunctory tasks. He advises starting small and gradually building these practices into one's daily routine. The ultimate goal is to transform one's life through sustained and intentional practice, allowing the apprentice to live in alignment with the teachings and example of Jesus.

KEY TAKEAWAYS

These key takeaways underscore the practical and relational nature of discipleship, encouraging believers to actively engage in the process of becoming more like Jesus through intentional practice and community support.

- Comer emphasizes that being a disciple of Jesus is akin to being an apprentice. This means learning from Jesus not only through His teachings but also by observing and emulating His way of life. Apprenticeship involves a hands-on approach, practicing what Jesus did in real-life situations.

- The chapter highlights the importance of imitating Jesus' spiritual disciplines, such as prayer, fasting, solitude, and service. These practices are essential for spiritual growth and becoming more like Jesus. Comer encourages readers to incorporate these disciplines into their daily routines to deepen their relationship with Him.

- Comer discusses how apprenticeship to Jesus leads to holistic transformation. This involves a change not just in behavior but in character, thought patterns, and emotions. By living like Jesus, disciples undergo a comprehensive transformation that affects every aspect of their lives.

- The chapter stresses the role of community in the apprenticeship journey. Being part of a supportive and accountable community helps disciples stay committed to their practices and provides encouragement and correction. Comer underscores that following Jesus is not a solo endeavor but a communal one.

- Comer provides practical steps for becoming an apprentice of Jesus. This includes setting specific goals for spiritual disciplines, finding mentors or spiritual directors, and actively seeking ways to serve others as Jesus did. These steps help to ground the lofty ideals of discipleship in actionable, everyday practices.

EXERCISES/PROMPTS: REFLECTING ON APPRENTICESHIP TO JESUS

Use these prompts to reflect deeply on what it means to be an apprentice to Jesus and to plan practical steps for living out His teachings in your daily life.

Understanding Apprenticeship

Reflect on the concept of being an apprentice to Jesus. What does this mean to you personally? How does viewing discipleship as an apprenticeship change your approach to following Jesus?

Write about a specific area in your life where you feel called to learn from and emulate Jesus more closely. How can you approach this area with the mindset of an apprentice?

Imitating Jesus' Practices

Choose one of Jesus' spiritual disciplines (prayer, fasting, solitude, service, etc.) that you would like to incorporate more into your life. Why did you choose this particular practice?

Develop a plan to integrate this discipline into your daily or weekly routine. What specific steps will you take to make this practice a regular part of your life?

Holistic Transformation

Reflect on a time when practicing a spiritual discipline led to a noticeable change in your character, thoughts, or emotions. What was the practice, and how did it transform you?

Identify an area of your life where you desire holistic transformation. How can you invite Jesus into this area and allow His teachings and example to guide your growth?

_____

_____

_____

_____

_____

_____

_____

_____

_____

_____

_____

_____

_____

_____

_____

_____

Community and Accountability

Think about your current community. How does it support your journey as an apprentice of Jesus? Are there ways you can deepen your connections and accountability within this community?

Write about a person or a group who could act as mentors or accountability partners in your discipleship journey. How can you approach them, and what role would you like them to play in your spiritual growth?

Practical Steps

Set one specific goal for your apprenticeship to Jesus in the coming month. This could be a new spiritual discipline, a service project, or a commitment to regular prayer or scripture reading.

Write down the steps you will take to achieve this goal. What resources, support, or changes in your routine will you need? How will you measure your progress and stay motivated?

CHAPTER 3
GOAL #1: BE WITH JESUS

SUMMARY

In the chapter "Goal #1: Be with Jesus" from "Practicing the Way" by John Mark Comer, the author emphasizes the foundational goal of Christian discipleship: to be with Jesus. Comer stresses that the essence of being an apprentice of Jesus involves cultivating an intimate, ongoing relationship with Him. This is not just about engaging in religious activities or accumulating knowledge but about fostering a deep, personal connection that transforms every aspect of life. Comer draws from the biblical concept of abiding in Jesus, urging readers to make space in their daily routines to experience His presence.

Comer provides practical advice on how to achieve this goal, highlighting the importance of developing spiritual habits that integrate Jesus into every moment of daily life. He suggests starting with small, manageable practices rather than overwhelming oneself with unrealistic expectations. For example, instead of aiming for long periods of prayer initially, one might begin with a few minutes a day. The key is consistency and gradual growth in one's relationship with Jesus. Comer also encourages practices like solitude, Sabbath, and community, which help create environments conducive to being with Jesus regularly.

The chapter underscores that the reward for following Jesus is not merely spiritual knowledge or moral improvement but Jesus Himself. Comer insists that the ultimate benefit of discipleship is the transformation that comes from being in constant communion with Jesus, experiencing His love, peace, and guidance in every aspect of life. This approach sets the foundation for the subsequent goals of becoming like Jesus and doing what He did, as it all starts with being deeply connected to Him.

KEY TAKEAWAYS

These takeaways focus on creating intentional habits and practices that foster a close and personal relationship with Jesus, emphasizing the need for dedicated time, solitude, prayer, mindfulness, scripture engagement, and Sabbath rest.

- Prioritizing time alone with God, away from distractions, to cultivate an intimate relationship with Jesus. This involves setting aside regular periods for solitude and silence, following Jesus' example of withdrawing to quiet places to pray.

- Viewing prayer not just as a ritual but as an ongoing conversation with Jesus. This includes both speaking to God and listening for His voice, fostering a deeper connection and understanding of His will.

- Inviting Jesus into all aspects of daily life, not just during designated prayer times. This means being aware of His presence throughout the day, in every activity, and seeking to live in constant communion with Him.

- Engaging deeply with the Bible, not just reading it but meditating on its truths. This practice helps believers to hear God's voice and internalize His teachings, making His words a living part of their daily lives.

- Observing the Sabbath as a time to rest and reconnect with God. Comer emphasizes the importance of setting aside a day for rest, reflection, and worship, following the rhythm established by God in creation.

- Developing a lifestyle of worship that goes beyond singing songs to include gratitude, adoration, and reverence for God in all things. This helps to keep the focus on Jesus and fosters a heart that delights in His presence.

EXERCISES/PROMPTS: REFLECTING ON SOLITUDE AND PRESENCE WITH JESUS

Use the following journal prompts to deepen your understanding of what it means to be with Jesus and to integrate these practices into your daily life.

Solitude and Silence

Describe a time when you felt closest to Jesus during a moment of solitude. What did you do during that time? How did you sense His presence?

How can you create more intentional times of solitude and silence in your daily routine? List some practical steps you can take to make this a regular practice.

Prayer as Communication

Reflect on your current prayer life. How do you communicate with Jesus? How do you listen for His voice?

Write down a prayer, inviting Jesus to speak to you. Afterward, spend a few minutes in silence, attentively listening for His response. Record any thoughts or impressions you receive.

Presence in Everyday Life

Think about a typical day in your life. In what moments do you feel most aware of Jesus' presence? In which moments do you feel least aware?

How can you remind yourself of Jesus' presence throughout your day? Consider setting specific times or cues to refocus your attention on Him.

Scripture Meditation

Choose a passage of scripture that speaks to you. Read it slowly and meditate on its meaning. How does this passage reveal Jesus' character and heart?

Write down any insights or revelations you receive from this meditation. How can you apply these insights to your daily life?

Sabbath Rest

Reflect on how you currently spend your Sabbath or a day of rest.
How does it help you reconnect with Jesus?

Plan an upcoming Sabbath day. What activities will you include to rest, reflect, and worship? How will you ensure this day is set apart for reconnecting with God?

Cultivating a Heart of Worship

List the things you are grateful for today. How do these blessings remind you of Jesus' love and provision?

_____

_____

_____

_____

_____

_____

_____

_____

_____

_____

_____

_____

_____

_____

_____

_____

Spend a few minutes in worship, expressing gratitude and adoration to Jesus. Record your thoughts and feelings during this time of worship.

CHAPTER 4
GOAL #2: BECOME LIKE HIM

SUMMARY

In the chapter "Goal #2: Become Like Him" from *Practicing the Way*, John Mark Comer emphasizes the transformative journey of becoming like Jesus. Comer argues that transformation into Christ-likeness is not a passive or instantaneous event but a deliberate and ongoing process. This transformation involves addressing the deep-seated issues of sin and the pre-existing formation from societal influences, personal habits, and relationships. Comer insists that mere willpower and increased biblical knowledge alone are insufficient for this transformation. Instead, he proposes a holistic approach that incorporates teaching, practice, community, and the Holy Spirit's work, which together facilitate genuine change over time, often through the trials and challenges of life.

Comer further explores the concept of spiritual formation, defining it as an intentional and structured process rather than an accidental occurrence. He outlines that becoming like Jesus requires a proactive engagement in spiritual disciplines and communal living that reflect Jesus' own practices. Comer stresses the importance of a "Rule of Life," a framework of daily and weekly rhythms that create space for spiritual growth and alignment with Jesus' teachings. This Rule of Life includes practices such as Sabbath, solitude, prayer, fasting, and acts of service, all designed to cultivate a deeper relationship with Jesus and foster character transformation.

The chapter concludes with a reminder that while the journey to become like Jesus is demanding and countercultural, it is profoundly rewarding. Comer encourages readers to embrace this transformative journey not as a checklist of duties but as a pathway to embodying the life and love of Jesus in practical, everyday ways. This transformation leads to living out the gospel authentically and effectively, impacting not just the individual but the broader community and world. Thus, Comer calls believers to commit to this lifelong process of becoming like Jesus, understanding that true spiritual maturity and fulfillment lie in this pursuit.

KEY TAKEAWAYS

These takeaways underscore the holistic and dynamic nature of spiritual growth, emphasizing both our active participation and reliance on God's transforming power.

- Comer emphasizes that becoming like Jesus starts with inner transformation. It's not just about external behavior but about allowing Jesus to change our hearts, minds, and desires from the inside out.

- Engaging in spiritual disciplines is crucial for transformation. Comer highlights practices such as prayer, fasting, meditation on scripture, and community involvement as ways to shape our inner lives to reflect Jesus' character.

- Comer discusses the importance of renewing our minds by immersing ourselves in God's truth. By regularly reading and meditating on scripture, we can align our thoughts with God's thoughts and cultivate a Christ-like mindset.

- Becoming like Jesus involves developing Christ-like character traits such as love, joy, peace, patience, kindness, goodness, faithfulness, gentleness, and self-control. Comer encourages readers to consciously practice these virtues in their daily lives.

- Comer addresses the necessity of confronting and dealing with sin in our lives. He advocates for regular self-examination, confession, and repentance as essential practices for anyone serious about becoming like Jesus.

- The chapter highlights the role of a Christian community in our transformation. Being part of a supportive and accountable community helps us grow and stay committed to the journey of becoming like Jesus.

- Comer emphasizes that true transformation is the work of the Holy Spirit. While we engage in practices that position us for growth, it is ultimately the Holy Spirit who brings about deep and lasting change.

- Finally, Comer reminds readers that becoming like Jesus is a lifelong process. It requires patience, perseverance, and a long-term commitment to continually growing and maturing in our faith and character.

EXERCISES/PROMPTS: REFLECTING ON BECOMING LIKE JESUS

Use these prompts to deeply engage with the process of becoming more like Jesus, reflecting on practical steps and seeking the Holy Spirit's guidance in your transformation.

Inner Transformation

Reflect on areas in your life where you feel Jesus is calling you to deeper inner transformation. What desires, attitudes, or thoughts need to be aligned more closely with His?

Write about a specific situation where you experienced a change in your heart or mind that brought you closer to the character of Jesus. What sparked this change, and how did it impact you?

Spiritual Disciplines

Choose one spiritual discipline (prayer, fasting, scripture meditation, etc.) that you want to focus on this week. Why did you choose this discipline, and how do you hope it will help you become more like Jesus?

Develop a practical plan for incorporating this discipline into your daily routine. What specific actions will you take to ensure you stay committed?

Renewing the Mind

Reflect on a passage of scripture that has recently impacted you. How does this passage help renew your mind and align your thoughts with God's truth?

Write about any negative thought patterns you struggle with. How can you counter these with the truths found in scripture?

Character Formation

Identify one Christ-like character trait (love, joy, peace, patience, kindness, goodness, faithfulness, gentleness, or self-control) that you want to develop more in your life. Why is this trait important to you?

Describe a practical way you can practice this trait in your daily interactions. How will you remind yourself to embody this character trait?

Dealing with Sin

Reflect on a sin or bad habit that you need to confront. Why is it important for your spiritual growth to address this issue?

Write a prayer of confession and repentance, asking for God's help to overcome this sin. What steps can you take to avoid falling back into this habit?

Community Support

Think about the role of community in your spiritual journey. How has your Christian community supported you in becoming more like Jesus?

Identify a person or a group in your community who can hold you accountable and encourage you in your journey. How can you actively seek their support?

The Role of the Holy Spirit

Reflect on how you have experienced the work of the Holy Spirit in your life. How has the Holy Spirit helped you in your journey to become more like Jesus?

Write a prayer asking the Holy Spirit to continue transforming you. What specific areas of your life do you want the Holy Spirit to work on?

Lifelong Process

Acknowledge that becoming like Jesus is a lifelong process. Reflect on your journey so far—how have you grown, and what are the areas you still need to work on?

Set long-term spiritual growth goals. What are the next steps you want to take in your journey to become more like Jesus over the next year?

CHAPTER 5
GOAL #3: DO AS HE DID

SUMMARY

In "Goal #3: Do as He Did" from "Practicing the Way," John Mark Comer emphasizes that the ultimate goal of being an apprentice of Jesus is to emulate His actions. Comer highlights the importance of continuing Jesus' work on earth by engaging in activities such as healing the sick, praying for the lost, and extending hospitality to those far from God. He suggests that our everyday actions should reflect what Jesus would do if He were in our place, thereby making our lives a testament to His teachings and actions.

Comer categorizes Jesus' actions into three primary areas: hospitality, preaching the gospel, and demonstrating the gospel. He explains that much of Jesus' ministry was relational, often involving meals and personal interactions, which created opportunities to share the gospel in a natural and impactful way. Preaching the gospel, according to Comer, involves joining in where God is already working, sharing personal testimonies, and living a life that visibly reflects God's love and principles. Demonstrating the gospel encompasses healing, deliverance, prophecy, and justice, showing the transformative power of Jesus' message through tangible actions.

To practically apply these principles, Comer suggests creating a "Rule of Life," a structured set of practices and rhythms that help align one's life with the goals of being with Jesus, becoming like Him, and doing as He did. He emphasizes the need for community in this process, as transformation is supported and enriched by shared practices and mutual accountability. This approach not only aids in personal spiritual growth but also enhances the collective witness of a community living out the teachings of Jesus.

KEY TAKEAWAYS

These takeaways highlight the active, service-oriented, and compassionate nature of following Jesus, encouraging believers to live out their faith through tangible actions that mirror the life and ministry of Jesus.

- Comer emphasizes the importance of not only believing in Jesus but also actively doing what He did. This includes practices like healing the sick, serving the poor, and proclaiming the good news, following the example set by Jesus.

- The chapter highlights hospitality as a significant practice of Jesus. Comer encourages believers to open their homes and lives to others, showing kindness and generosity to friends, strangers, and those in need.

- Serving others is a core aspect of Jesus' ministry. Comer stresses the need for Christians to engage in practical acts of service, reflecting Jesus' humility and love by meeting the physical and spiritual needs of others.

- Comer discusses the importance of proclaiming the Kingdom of God. This involves sharing the gospel and teaching others about Jesus' life and message, making disciples as Jesus commanded.

- The chapter underscores the need to cultivate compassion, as Jesus did. This means developing empathy for the marginalized, oppressed, and hurting, and taking concrete steps to alleviate their suffering and advocate for justice.

- Comer calls for radical obedience to Jesus' teachings and commands. This involves making sometimes difficult and counter-cultural choices that align with the values of the Kingdom of God, demonstrating a commitment to live out Jesus' teachings in everyday life.

EXERCISES/PROMPTS: REFLECTING ON DOING AS JESUS DID

Use these prompts to deeply engage with the teachings of Jesus and to plan practical steps for living out His example in your everyday life.

Emulating Jesus' Actions

Reflect on specific actions Jesus took during His ministry that you feel called to emulate. Which of Jesus' practices (healing, serving, teaching, etc.) resonate most with you, and why?

_____

_____

_____

_____

_____

_____

_____

_____

_____

_____

Write about one way you can incorporate this practice into your life this week. What steps will you take to start doing this?

Practicing Hospitality

Consider how you can practice hospitality in your current circumstances. Who in your life could benefit from an invitation into your home or a gesture of kindness?

Plan an act of hospitality you will do this week. Describe what you will do, who you will invite or serve, and how you hope it will reflect Jesus' love.

Engaging in Acts of Service

Reflect on recent opportunities you've had to serve others. How did these experiences make you feel, and what did you learn about yourself and about God through them?

Identify a specific act of service you can commit to this month. How will you serve, and who will you serve? Write about the impact you hope to have.

Proclaiming the Kingdom

Think about how you can share the message of the Kingdom of God in your daily life. What are some natural ways you can talk about your faith with others?

Write a short plan for a conversation or an action that will allow you to share the gospel or demonstrate the values of the Kingdom of God. How will you approach this?

Cultivating Compassion

Reflect on an area of your life where you feel called to show more compassion. Who in your community or beyond is in need of love and support?

_____

_____

_____

_____

_____

_____

_____

_____

_____

_____

_____

_____

_____

_____

Describe a specific action you will take to demonstrate compassion this week. How can you provide support or advocate for someone who is marginalized or hurting?

Living with Radical Obedience

Consider what radical obedience to Jesus looks like for you. Are there any areas of your life where you struggle to follow His teachings fully?

Write a prayer asking for strength and courage to live out Jesus' teachings with radical obedience. Commit to one specific change you will make to align your life more closely with His commands.

CHAPTER 6
HOW? A RULE OF LIFE

SUMMARY

In the chapter "How? A Rule of Life" from John Mark Comer's book "Practicing the Way," Comer explains the concept of a Rule of Life as a framework for spiritual formation. A Rule of Life is a set of practices and relational rhythms designed to create space for individuals to be with Jesus, become like Him, and do as He did. Comer likens this rule to a trellis in a vineyard, which supports and guides the growth of a vine. The Rule of Life is intended to organize one's life around abiding in Jesus, helping believers align their daily activities with their spiritual values and goals.

Comer emphasizes that a Rule of Life should be flexible and tailored to an individual's unique personality, season of life, and stage of discipleship. He advises starting small with manageable goals to avoid discouragement and suggests specific practices such as morning prayer, Sabbath, and regular rest. Comer stresses that the Rule of Life is a dynamic document that should evolve over time to remain life-giving and supportive of one's spiritual journey. It is not a rigid set of rules but a means to foster growth and freedom in one's relationship with God.

To craft a Rule of Life, Comer recommends considering practical and concrete practices that can be incorporated into daily routines. He also highlights the importance of balancing structured practices with spontaneity to keep the rule from becoming a burdensome obligation. The ultimate goal of a Rule of Life is to help believers stay connected to Jesus and become more like Him, transforming their lives and enabling them to bear much fruit in their spiritual journey.

KEY TAKEAWAYS

These takeaways provide a comprehensive understanding of how to create and implement a Rule of Life that supports intentional spiritual growth and alignment with the way of Jesus.

- Comer defines a "Rule of Life" as a set of spiritual practices and rhythms that help individuals live in alignment with their values and priorities, specifically to abide in Jesus and follow His way.

- The purpose of a Rule of Life is to create a framework that fosters spiritual growth and transformation. It is a tool to help Christians intentionally structure their lives around the teachings and practices of Jesus.

- A Rule of Life is not a one-size-fits-all approach; it should be personalized to fit each individual's life stage, personality, and spiritual needs. It is meant to be flexible and adaptable rather than rigid and legalistic.

- Comer emphasizes that a Rule of Life should encompass all areas of life, including spiritual, relational, physical, and vocational aspects. This holistic approach ensures balanced growth and integration of faith into every part of life.

- The chapter discusses the importance of establishing rhythms that include daily, weekly, and seasonal practices. These rhythms create a sustainable pattern of life that supports ongoing spiritual development.

- Comer highlights the role of community in developing and maintaining a Rule of Life. Sharing one's rule with trusted friends or mentors provides accountability, encouragement, and support.

- Regularly reviewing and adjusting the Rule of Life is crucial. This practice ensures that it remains relevant and effective, allowing for changes based on personal growth, new insights, and life circumstances.

- Comer outlines core practices to include in a Rule of Life, such as prayer, scripture reading, Sabbath rest, simplicity, and hospitality. Integrating these practices helps believers stay connected to Jesus and live out His teachings daily.

- The chapter provides practical advice on how to implement a Rule of Life, including starting small, being realistic, and gradually incorporating new practices. Comer stresses the importance of patience and perseverance in developing a sustainable Rule of Life.

EXERCISES/PROMPTS: CREATING AND LIVING BY A RULE OF LIFE

Use these prompts to thoughtfully create and implement a Rule of Life that supports intentional spiritual growth, holistic living, and alignment with the teachings of Jesus.

Defining Your Rule of Life

Reflect on what a "Rule of Life" means to you. How can establishing a Rule of Life help you align your daily routines with your spiritual values and goals?

_____

_____

_____

_____

_____

_____

_____

_____

_____

_____

_____

Write down your initial thoughts on what practices and rhythms you want to include in your Rule of Life. Consider spiritual disciplines, relational commitments, physical well-being, and vocational goals.

Personalization and Flexibility

Think about how your Rule of Life can be personalized to fit your unique life stage, personality, and spiritual needs. What aspects of your life require flexibility in your spiritual practices?

Draft a Rule of Life that is adaptable and realistic for you. Include daily, weekly, and seasonal rhythms that support your spiritual growth while allowing for adjustments as needed.

Holistic Integration

Reflect on how your Rule of Life can encompass all areas of your life. How can you ensure that your spiritual, relational, physical, and vocational aspects are integrated into your Rule of Life?

Write a plan for how you will balance these different areas. Identify specific practices or habits that will help you maintain a holistic approach to your spiritual journey.

Core Practices

Identify core spiritual practices that are essential for your Rule of Life, such as prayer, scripture reading, Sabbath rest, simplicity, and hospitality. Why are these practices important to you?

Describe how you will incorporate each of these core practices into your daily or weekly routine. What specific actions will you take to prioritize these disciplines?

Community and Accountability

Reflect on the role of community in your spiritual journey. How can sharing your Rule of Life with trusted friends or mentors provide accountability, encouragement, and support?

Write about how you will engage your community in your Rule of Life. Consider who you can share your rule with, and how you will seek their support and feedback.

Review and Adjustment

Consider the importance of regularly reviewing and adjusting your Rule of Life. How will you ensure that your rule remains relevant and effective over time?

Plan a regular review schedule for your Rule of Life. Write about how you will evaluate your progress and make necessary adjustments based on personal growth, new insights, and changing circumstances.

Intentional Living

Reflect on how creating a Rule of Life can help you live more intentionally. What changes do you hope to see in your daily routines and overall lifestyle as a result of implementing your Rule of Life?

Write a vision statement for your Rule of Life. Describe the kind of person you want to become and how your Rule of Life will help you achieve this vision.

Practical Implementation

Think about the practical steps needed to implement your Rule of Life. How will you start small, be realistic, and gradually incorporate new practices into your routine?

Write a step-by-step plan for implementing your Rule of Life. Consider what resources, tools, or reminders you will need to stay committed and motivated in this journey.

CHAPTER 7
TAKE UP YOUR CROSS

SUMMARY

In the chapter "Take Up Your Cross" from John Mark Comer's book "Practicing the Way," the author delves into the concept of self-denial as central to the Christian faith. Comer emphasizes that in contemporary society, where self-fulfillment and individualism are highly valued, the idea of self-denial and taking up one's cross is counter-cultural and often misunderstood. He explains that following Jesus involves a willingness to deny oneself and embrace a lifestyle of sacrificial love, mirroring Jesus' own journey to the cross.

Comer argues that the cross, historically a symbol of suffering and death, has lost much of its profound meaning in modern times. He calls readers to reclaim the depth of this symbol by truly understanding what it means to follow Jesus. This entails a daily commitment to live out the values and teachings of Jesus, which often means going against the grain of societal norms that prioritize personal happiness and success over spiritual growth and communal well-being.

The chapter also discusses the practical implications of this commitment. Comer suggests that taking up one's cross involves making deliberate choices that reflect the teachings of Jesus, such as showing compassion, seeking justice, and practicing forgiveness. By doing so, believers participate in the transformative power of the cross, not just as a historical event but as a living, active force in their lives. This transformative journey is marked by a profound trust in God's love and a willingness to surrender control, leading to true freedom and joy.

KEY TAKEAWAYS

These takeaways underscore the challenging yet deeply transformative nature of following Jesus, calling believers to a life of sacrifice, self-denial, and counter-cultural living.

- Comer emphasizes that taking up one's cross involves embracing the sacrifices and sufferings inherent in following Jesus. This means being willing to endure hardship, rejection, and discomfort for the sake of the gospel, reflecting Jesus' own journey of self-denial and suffering.

- The chapter highlights the necessity of dying to self, which involves letting go of personal ambitions, desires, and ego. This self-denial allows believers to fully surrender to God's will, prioritizing His purposes over their own and fostering a deeper, more authentic discipleship.

- Comer discusses the counter-cultural nature of taking up one's cross. Following Jesus often means living in ways that contrast sharply with societal norms and values, such as prioritizing service over power, generosity over accumulation, and humility over pride. This radical way of living serves as a powerful witness to the transformative power of the gospel.

EXERCISES/PROMPTS: REFLECTING ON TAKING UP YOUR CROSS

Use these prompts to reflect deeply on the personal implications of taking up your cross and to plan practical steps for living out this challenging yet transformative aspect of following Jesus.

Embracing Sacrifice and Suffering

Reflect on a time in your life when following Jesus required you to make a significant sacrifice or endure suffering. How did this experience shape your faith and relationship with God?

_____

_____

_____

_____

_____

_____

_____

_____

_____

_____

_____

_____

Identify an area of your life where you sense God calling you to embrace sacrifice or endure hardship for His sake. What steps can you take to respond to this call with faith and obedience?

Dying to Self

Consider aspects of your personal ambitions, desires, or ego that you need to let go of to follow Jesus more closely. What are these areas, and why is it challenging to surrender them?

Write a prayer of surrender, asking God to help you die to self and align your desires with His will. How can you practice self-denial in your daily life to foster a deeper discipleship?

Living Counter-Culturally

Reflect on ways in which living as a disciple of Jesus sets you apart from societal norms and values. How does this counter-cultural living manifest in your choices, relationships, and lifestyle?

Identify one specific area where you feel called to live more counter-culturally. What practical steps can you take to prioritize Jesus' values over societal expectations, and how can this serve as a witness to others?

CHAPTER 8
ADDITIONAL REFLECTIVE EXERCISES

Utilizing reflective exercises offers a profound way to deepen understanding and practice the teachings from "Practicing the Way: Be with Jesus. Become like him. Do as he did." by John Mark Comer.

This chapter introduces various methods designed to cultivate spiritual growth, enhance mindfulness, and foster a closer connection with God through intentional reflection. Each exercise invites readers to engage in practices that transcend traditional prayer and scripture study, encouraging a more intimate and transformative experience of faith.

EXERCISE: CONTEMPLATIVE PRAYER

Contemplative prayer offers a profound way to deepen one's spiritual connection and cultivate a closer relationship with God. This practice involves sitting in silent awareness of God's presence, an act that transcends the traditional, verbal forms of prayer that many are accustomed to.

By engaging in contemplative prayer, individuals can open themselves to a more profound experience of divine companionship, embodying the essence of being with Jesus as taught in 'Practicing the Way.'

The consistent practice of contemplative prayer substantially enhances one's sense of spiritual groundedness. When practiced regularly, it promotes a steady rhythm of stepping back from daily life's demands to center oneself in God's presence.

Over time, this practice cultivates a peaceful and resilient spirit, better equipped to navigate life's challenges with grace and faith. Such resilience and peace stem from knowing deeply that one is continuously seen and loved by God.

This practice also strengthens personal discipline. Committing to a daily practice, even when life feels hectic, reinforces the priority of one's spiritual well-being. Over time, consistent engagement with contemplative prayer reconfigures one's day-to-day priorities, shifting focus towards a deeper communion with God.

Establishing a daily routine ensures that this sacred practice becomes an integral part of one's life. Selecting a specific time and place dedicated to this prayer helps in forming a habit, making it easier to return to this reflective state regularly.

Use the following space to write down your plan for committing to consistent, contemplative prayer. This should include the specific time and place and can also include the duration. You can also use this space to write down any thoughts or feelings you have had after committing to this practice. Describe the context, your feelings, and how you believe Jesus was moving or speaking to you in those moments.

EXERCISE: SCRIPTURE MEDITATION

Integrating biblical teachings into one's life through meditation can transform our daily experiences and relationship with God. One effective method is scripture meditation, which involves choosing a passage of scripture and reflecting on it deeply throughout the day.

This practice encourages the reader to slow down and allow God's word to sink in rather than skimming quickly through texts. Reflecting on a chosen passage helps the reader connect more intimately with the teachings and understand its implications in everyday scenarios.

For instance, consider selecting a verse from Psalms or Proverbs. Throughout your day, return your thoughts to this verse during quiet moments such as commutes, breaks, or before sleep. This sustained reflection nurtures a deeper comprehension and appreciation of the scripture. Gradually, you begin to see connections between the passage and your life's circumstances, making the Bible's wisdom an active part of your decision-making and behavior.

Use the following space to write down the scriptures you chose and what connections to your current life circumstances you saw for each one.

EXERCISE: SCRIPTURE MEMORIZATION

Another critical aspect of integrating biblical teachings is memorizing and internalizing key verses. By committing verses to memory, one can recall them during times of need or when making decisions, offering guidance and comfort. Memorized scripture acts like a spiritual toolbox, ready to be accessed whenever required. This practice not only strengthens one's knowledge of the Bible but also fortifies the spirit during trials.

For example, memorizing Philippians 4:13, "I can do all this through him who gives me strength," provides encouragement and resilience in difficult times. When faced with uncertainty or fear, recalling such a verse can shift focus from personal limitations to divine support, fostering a sense of empowerment and trust in God's plan.

Incorporating memory work into daily routines can start small, with just one verse a week. Over time, these verses accumulate, enriching the mind and heart. Regularly revisiting and rehearsing these scriptures ensures they remain fresh and accessible, becoming an intrinsic part of your spiritual journey. With this repetition, you will also find it reveals new layers of meaning and application that might be missed during the first reading.

Effective meditation involves specific steps to maximize its benefits.

First, select a scripture passage that speaks to your current needs or challenges. This relevance makes the meditation more impactful, as the chosen words resonate closely with your life situation. Taking time to pray for discernment in selecting the right passage ensures that the meditation aligns with God's guidance for your growth.

Next, find a quiet place free from distractions which allows for focused and uninterrupted reflection. Creating a dedicated space for this purpose can enhance concentration and make the practice more meaningful. Whether it's a corner of your home, a park bench, or a peaceful spot in a library, the environment plays a crucial role in setting the tone for deep meditation.

Repetition is another key element. Rehearse the passage mentally and verbally, letting its words soak into your consciousness. This repetition solidifies the scripture in your memory and highlights different facets of its meaning each time you contemplate it. It's akin to polishing a gem; the more you turn it over and study it, the more brilliant it becomes.

Lastly, listen for God's voice. Allow moments of silence and stillness to invite divine inspiration and insight. While meditation involves active thinking and memorization, the listening phase requires you to open your heart and mind to God's whisper. This receptive state fosters a two-way connection, transforming meditation from a mechanical activity into a heartfelt communion with the divine.

Use the following space to write down the scriptures you chose to commit to memory first. You can also write down your thoughts and what your learned from them during contemplation.

EXERCISE: ACTS OF KINDNESS AND COMMUNITY SERVICE

Developing a plan to emulate Jesus' humility, compassion, and forgiveness is pivotal. Start by setting specific, achievable goals. For example, commit to acts of kindness daily, such as helping a neighbor or being patient with a challenging coworker. Deliberately practicing these virtues helps embed them into your habits and interactions. Drawing inspiration from scripture can also guide you. Verses highlighting Jesus' humility, like Philippians 2:3-8, can be meditated upon regularly to reinforce these values.

Use the following space to write down your goals for committing acts of kindness daily.

Engaging in community service is another tangible way to apply Jesus' teachings. Volunteering at local shelters, participating in food drives, or simply offering help to neighbors in need embodies Jesus' call to serve others. These acts not only benefit the recipients but also cultivate a spirit of generosity and empathy within you, drawing you closer to living like Jesus.

Service opportunities often bring you face-to-face with diverse communities, including those marginalized or overlooked. Interacting with people from different backgrounds can broaden your perspective and deepen your understanding of Jesus' inclusive love. Just as Jesus associated with society's outcasts, serving in varied communities teaches humility and breaks down prejudices, fostering a genuine sense of unity and compassion.

Additionally, community service strengthens your connection with others on the same path. Serving alongside likeminded individuals provides support and fosters a collective effort toward a common goal. This camaraderie enhances your spiritual growth and keeps you motivated to live out Jesus' teachings actively.

Use the following space to write down how you plan to engage in community service.

EXERCISE: REGULAR REFLECTION

Consider setting aside time weekly or monthly to review what you have written in this workbook. Reflect on any patterns or recurring themes that may emerge from these reflections. You might notice that certain activities, places, or even times of day are more conducive to experiencing Jesus' presence.

Use these insights to guide your future contemplative practices and align your daily rhythms more closely with what helps you feel connected to Him. Sharing these documented experiences with a trusted friend or spiritual mentor can also offer additional perspectives and encouragement.

This consistent review ensures continuous growth and alignment with Jesus' teachings.

Use the following space to write down any observations you have noticed as you look back on your progress. If you shared these experiences with a friend or mentor, you can also write down any insights you gained from this.

CONCLUSION

As you reach the end of this workbook, take a moment to reflect on the journey you've embarked upon. You've delved into practical exercises aimed at integrating the teachings from John Mark Comer's "Practicing the Way" into your daily life. These exercises are designed not just to offer temporary inspiration but to cultivate lasting transformation in your spiritual journey.

Throughout these chapters, you've explored foundational aspects of being with Jesus, becoming like Him, and doing as He did. You've discovered practical ways to develop a personal relationship with Jesus through scripture reading, prayer, solitude, and worship. You've learned about character transformation by embracing humility, patience, kindness, and self-control. You've examined how to engage in kingdom work, serving others, sharing faith naturally, and living out justice and mercy. All of these practices contribute to building a Rule of Life tailored to your specific needs and circumstances.

Your journey started with understanding the essence of "Practicing the Way," recognizing the importance of aligning your daily routines with spiritual goals. You were encouraged to set the stage for deeper discipleship, laying down a robust foundation for a meaningful and transformative relationship with Jesus. Each day presents an opportunity to integrate spiritual practices into your regular activities, fostering an environment where growth can flourish.

Engaging with the Word—actively meditating on scripture, creating a habit of daily Bible reading, and incorporating accountability—has equipped you to draw closer to Jesus. Equally important has been your exploration of prayer as a two-way conversation, enriching your connection with God through various prayer methods and maintaining consistency in your prayer life.

Solitude and silence have offered moments of deep reflection, allowing distractions to fade away and creating space for an intimate encounter with Jesus. This quiet time has been instrumental in listening for God's voice and cultivating mindfulness. Similarly, incorporating worship into your daily routines has fostered a heart full of gratitude and reverence, transforming ordinary moments into acts of devotion.

Character transformation came next. Emulating Jesus' humility by practicing servanthood, nurturing a teachable spirit, and extending grace and forgiveness has shown that true greatness lies in putting others first. Patience has taught you to trust in God's timing, practice compassion, and develop resilience against life's challenges.

Kindness has been another cornerstone. Generosity, compassion, and hospitality reflect God's selfless love and are powerful tools for embodying Christ's teachings. Finally, developing self-control has enabled you to resist temptations, manage emotions thoughtfully, and cultivate spiritual discipline.

Doing as Jesus did means engaging actively in kingdom work. Recognizing your unique calling allows you to serve with purpose and collaborate for greater impact. Local community service has given you a chance to make a tangible difference, while authentic witnessing turns everyday interactions into opportunities for sharing faith.

Living out justice and mercy is integral to kingdom work. Advocating for the marginalized, practicing mercy, living with integrity, and persevering in righteousness collectively demonstrate the transformative power of faith in action.

Creating a Rule of Life involves assessing your current practices, setting attainable spiritual goals, exploring various disciplines, and regularly reviewing and refining your plan. This structured approach ensures sustained spiritual growth, adapting to different life seasons, and emphasizing flexibility and resilience.

Overcoming obstacles is part of the journey. Recognize signs of spiritual stagnation, manage time effectively, handle doubt and dryness with grace, and seek accountability and support. This chapter empowers you to navigate through difficulties and continue progressing in your spiritual walk.

The role of community has been highlighted as crucial for supporting spiritual practice and growth. Small groups, corporate worship, finding mentors, and encouraging others enrich your faith journey, providing mutual support, wisdom, and companionship.

Finally, sustaining lifelong faithfulness requires reflecting on spiritual progress, continuously deepening habits, adapting practices to different life phases, and leaving a legacy of faith. Regular introspection ensures ongoing growth, while embracing advanced spiritual disciplines expands your horizons. Adaptability cultivates resilience, and modeling a faithful life inspires future generations.

Now, as you contemplate these learnings, consider how each chapter has impacted your relationship with God. Reflect on the ways in which you've grown and the areas that still need nurturing. Personalize your Rule of Life further, making necessary adjustments to ensure it aligns with your evolving spiritual needs and goals.

Imagine the transformation that will unfold as you consistently incorporate these practices into your daily routine. Visualize the depth of your connection with Jesus growing stronger with each step you take. Even in moments of doubt or dryness, trust that God is with you, guiding and shaping you through every season.

Today, take concrete steps towards establishing a lasting commitment to these practices. Revisit your Rule of Life, review your progress, and set new goals if needed. Seek support from your community, engage in small groups, participate in corporate worship, and find mentors who can guide you.

Remember, this is not just a one-time endeavor but a lifelong pursuit. Your dedication to "Practicing the Way" will not only transform your own life but also ripple out to those around you. Through your actions, you become a testament to the love and grace of Jesus, inspiring others to embark on their own journeys of faith.

As you move forward, may your life be a continuous expression of devotion, reflecting the character of Jesus in all that you do. Embrace the journey with an open heart, trusting in God's guidance, and let your faith shine brightly as a beacon of hope and love in the world.

THANK YOU!

Thank you for joining us on this transformative trip with *Practicing the Way: Be with Jesus. Become Like Him. Do as He Did.* by John Mark Comer. We trust that you have found this guide to be helpful in your journey to truly follow Jesus Christ.

We kindly request that you take a few moments to provide your valuable feedback by writing your review. We appreciate your valuable insights and suggestions, which will greatly contribute to our ongoing efforts to enhance and customize our resources for the benefit of our readers.

May you continue to experience growth, satisfaction, and success as you journey towards becoming formed by Christ.

Best regards!

Made in the USA
Coppell, TX
07 September 2024